ROOTED

Six Spiritual Habits that Renew the Soul

TANYA C. INGRAM

ROOTED: Six Spiritual Habits that Renew the Soul. Copyright © by Tanya C. Ingram.

All rights reserved. Printed in the United States of America.

No part of this book may be used or reproduced in any manner whatsoever without written permission except in the case of brief quotations embodied in critical articles and reviews. Scripture is taken from the New American Standard Version of the Bible.

For information, address DW Creative Publishers, 5 Cowboys Way; Frisco, TX 75034.

DW Creative Publishers books may be purchased for business, educational, religious, or sales promotional use. For information, please email connect@dwcreativepublishers.com.

To connect with the author, Tanya C. Ingram, visit www.RootedtheBook.com.

FIRST EDITION

Cover design by: DW Creative Publishers

Interior design by: DW Creative Publishers

Editing by: DW Creative Publishers

PRINT BOOK: ISBN 978-1-952605-26-0

EBOOK: ISBN 978-1-952605-27-7

Library of Congress Control Number: 2023902984

TABLE OF CONTENTS

Introduction _____ 1

The Life of Jesus Christ _____ 3

Disciplines: A Closer Look _____ 5

Devotion to God – Contemplative Movement _____ 5
Virtue in Thought, Word, and Action – Holiness Movement ____ 5
Empowerment by the Spirit – Charismatic Movement _____ 6
Compassion for All People – Social Justice Movement _____ 7
Proclamation of the Good News – Evangelical Movement _____ 7
Harmony between Faith and Work – Uniting the Physical and Spiritual _____ 8

Day 1: Love for the Lost _____ 10

Day 2: God Cares for You _____ 13

Day 3: Asking the Right Questions _____ 16

Day 4: Compassion Sounds Like This _____ 19

Day 5: Seeing God Clearly _____ 22

Day 6: Speaking on My Behalf _____ 25

Day 7: All Things Are Working for Good _____ 28

Day 8: Appreciate the Rain _____ 31

Day 9: Stages of Grief _____ 34

Day 10: Good Trouble _____ 37

Day 11: God Is Present _____ 40

Day 12: An Unconventional Faith _____ 43

Day 13: I Know Who I Am	46
Day 14: The Power of Contentment	49
Day 15: Faith to Go Forward	52
Day 16: Because I'm Happy!	55
Day 17: My Living is not Vain	58
Day 18: Managing Stress	61
Day 19: A Good Work in You	64
Day 20: Praying in Discouraging Times	67
Day 21: A Good Response	70
Day 22: Power of Tears	73
Day 23: In the Right Place	76
Day 24: God is "There" With You	79
Day 25: Surviving the Storm	82
Day 26: Nature's Reminder	85
Day 27: Becoming More Merciful	88
Day 28: Little Graces All Around	91
Day 29: Using Your Gifts for Others	94
Day 30: God's Way to Get You to Move	97
Day 31: Living A Whole Life	100
Bibliography	103

INTRODUCTION

Life is filled with tension, challenges, and stress. These days we are often told we must always be "on" and have a solution or response for everything we face. Newsflash: That is impossible. "Staying ready so you don't have to get ready" is unrealistic and promises to leave you with anxiety, fatigue, and burnout.

Jesus had a full life and rigorous ministry. Even with the demands of human suffering, managing his own family dynamics, and the pressures that came from living in a diverse society with its political and economic injustices, Jesus found a way to connect with God and others. He was confident in His ministry and calling.

This book looks at how Jesus lived. The practices and habits that made Him successful are available to us today. You will find short daily devotionals that explain the spiritual practices of Christ and it will encourage you to meditate on a few short questions as you think about your life, its demands, and ways to thrive.

Often in life we find ourselves faced with challenges. Accepting Christ, serving in ministry, trying to be good, and meet the needs of others can place us under the weight of doubt, anxiety, and fear. This book is designed to draw you into deeper intimacy with God, shape your time while in His presence and aid you in developing practices that will evolve into daily habits. It is in these daily practices that we create strategies to care for the soul. In my own life, when I have taken the time to care for my soul and engaged in habits that renewed me, I was able to be more peaceful, productive, and content.

We all have strengths and weaknesses. I invite you to think about the areas you can grow in practicing your faith. Look forward to what God will do and how you will continue to grow as you pause to practice your faith and care for your soul.

Along with reading and reflection, my prayer is that you will take advantage of the graphics on each page by coloring. Yes, color in your book! We know that coloring is a great way to relieve stress and anxiety. Start reading today and through your time spent with God, it is my prayer that this devotional will remind you of God's profound and abiding love for you.

Proverbs 4:23 says, "Above all else, guard your heart, for everything you do flows from it."

THE LIFE OF JESUS CHRIST

From the life of Jesus Christ, six distinct areas emerge:

1. Devotion to God – the Contemplative Tradition. Jesus lived a life filled with prayer. He prayed and had private time with God often. Read Mark 14:32-36.

2. Virtue in thought, word, and action – the Holiness Tradition. Christ lived a spotless life. Read Matthew 4:1-11.

3. Empowerment by the Spirit – the Charismatic Tradition. Living a life in which the Holy Spirit guided the actions and course of Jesus' life. Read John 14:15-17.

4. Compassion toward all people – the Social Justice Tradition. Living a life that valued and protected the dignity of every human being. Read Micah 6:8.

5. Proclamation of the good news of the gospel – the Evangelical Tradition. Jesus' life was centered on the Scriptures. Read Luke 4:16-20.

6. Harmony between faith and work – the Incarnational Tradition. Jesus lived a life that infused faith, work, and service.

Action Taken	Tradition	Practice Living	Scripture	Exercises
Devotion to God	Contemplative	Living a prayer filled life	Mark 14:32-36; Luke 11:1	Pray Daily for 10 minutes. Keep a prayer journal Find a peaceful place to pray in the outdoors.
Virtue in action, speaking & thinking	Holiness	Living a virtuous life	Matthew 4:1-11, 1 Timothy 4:7-8	Spend a day without saying anything negative, foul or dishonest. Fast for 1 day.
Empowerment by the Spirit	Charismatic	Living a Spirit-empowered life	John 14:15-17; Ephesians 5:18-19	Ask God to develop the fruits of the Spirit in your life. Discover your spiritual gifts and start using them.
Compassion toward all people	Social Justice	Living a Compassionate Life	Amos 5:24; Matthew 25:31-36	Look at injustice and address one area by donating to a cause. Join a group that advocates for the homeless, immigrants or people of color. Take a stand against racism, sexism, homophobia and other phobias or societal evils.
Proclamation of the gospel	Evangelical	Living the Word-centered life	Luke 4:16-20, 42-44 and John 11:25-26	Memorize an unfamiliar Scripture. Think about this Scripture and share what you think or feel about it with someone.
Harmony between faith and work	Incarnational	Living a sacramental life	Luke 13:10-17; Corinthians 4:7	Bless your home. Pray for God's presence and peace in each room. Seek wisdom from God on how to show His love to those on your job, in school and where you volunteer.

Reference: Smith, James B., *A Spiritual Formation Workbook: Small Group Resources for Nurturing Christian Growth, A Revised Edition*. New York: Harper Collins, 1999.

DISCIPLINES

A CLOSER LOOK

Devotion to God – Contemplative Movement

God and the Contemplative Tradition

At the heart of each tradition of the Church is God. Jesus is "God with us," a physical presence to show us what God is like. His actions and words reveal God's nature to us. When we practice the prayer-filled life, we discover the tender love of God. Read the story of the prodigal son (Luke 15:11-32). When we accept God in this way, praying to Him becomes less of a chore and more of an inner desire to connect with our loving Father.

Virtue in Thought, Word, and Action – Holiness Movement

God and the Holiness Tradition

God cares about sin. The Bible makes it very clear that people of God can be free from the power of sin. What is sin? According to the Bible, sin is rejecting the commandments of God. Adam and Eve rejected God's command and ate the fruit; Jonah rejected God's command and ran away from his calling. Every time the commands of God were rejected, disaster followed.

Often, we think of God's commandments as rules that stop our happiness and make us feel guilt. Not so! The commands of God are given to us so we might live abundantly. Consider the Ten Commandments (Exodus 20:2-17), each commandment calls us to the blessed life, the pathway to true happiness. Holiness is something God wishes for us simply because it is the best way to live.

Empowerment by the Spirit – Charismatic Movement

God and the Charismatic Tradition

The Holy Spirit has been called the forgotten person of the Trinity. Since its beginning on the day of Pentecost, the Church has believed in one God, made up of three persons – "God the Father, God the Son, and God the Holy Spirit." Although the Holy Spirit is equal in the Trinity, He is often neglected. We pray to God the Father in the name and authority of Jesus, the Son but often forget the role of the Holy Spirit in our lives. However, the Holy Spirit is God, and in particular, God at work in the Christian.

The Holy Spirit continues and completes the work God the Father and God the Son have begun in the life of the believer. The Holy Spirit is the believer's advocate, helper, comforter and counselor. As believers we are temples in whom the Holy Spirit dwells.

In First Corinthians 3:16, we are empowered by the Spirit to share the gospel. In Galatians 5:22, we are admonished to bear the fruit of the gospel in our lives and to exercise special gifts that enable us to build the Church as outlined in Romans 12:6-8:1, 1 Corinthians 12-14:25 and Ephesians 4:11-13.

Compassion for All People – Social Justice Movement

God and the Social Justice Tradition

God cares deeply about how we treat one another. When asked which commandment in the law is greatest, Jesus responded, "You should love the Lord your God with all your heart, and with all your soul, and with all your mind. This is the greatest and first commandment. And a second is like it: you shall love your neighbor as yourself." On these two commandments hang all the law and the prophets (Matthew 22:37-40).

God gives us instructions, so we know how to act. The call to love one another is outlined in 1 John 4:11. The book of Proverbs 14:31 tells us, "Those who oppress the poor insult their Maker." If we could see the world through the eyes of God, we would look through a filter of compassion. God cares about our needs, hurts, and brokenness, but instead of judging us, God is ready to forgive, heal and restore us.

Jesus lived a life of compassion for "the least." He mended, cared for, and forgave those in need and yet his compassion never undermined his sense of justice. The whole idea of compassion is based on a keen awareness of the interdependence of all living beings, which are part of one another, and involved in one another.

Proclamation of the Good News – Evangelical Movement

God and the Evangelical Tradition

God uses three ways to reveal himself to us. He uses the written word, the living word and the spoken word. Most familiar, the Bible is used to communicate directly with God's people. The Bible is sacred. Christians know the Old and New Testaments as the written Word and hold it in high esteem because from them we learn about God.

Next is the living Word, Jesus Christ is God's clearest expression of himself and statement of his purpose. John 1:1 states, "In the beginning was the Word (the Logos), and the Word was with God, and the Word was God." As the Logos, Jesus reveals to us a God who creates, loves, heals, and understands. When we look into the face of Jesus, we see God. When we see Jesus' eyes radiate with compassion or hear his voice speak about justice, salvation and reconciliation, we experience God, because Jesus is God.

But it is the spoken word of God, the proclamation of the gospel that is at the core of the Word-centered life. The word is to be communicated; to have its meaning conveyed. At the core of the Word-centered life, every Christian is to use Scripture to connect with others. In talking about our faith, we speak the written word (the Bible) that talks about the living word (Jesus) so that hearers can establish a relationship with God. Every Christian is called to proclaim the gospel to those who have not heard it. So, if faith comes from what is heard and what is heard comes through the word of Christ (Romans 10:17) who does the proclaiming? Believers are the witnesses to the person of Jesus Christ whose story resides in the Bible. We are to proclaim the good news of God's Word.

Harmony between Faith and Work - Uniting the Physical and Spiritual

God and the Incarnational Tradition

As physical beings, we find it easy to focus on the material things we can see and touch. We need food to live; we put clothes on our bodies; and if we close our finger in the car door, we feel pain and take medicine. However, this can challenge us when we start to explore the world of the spirit. We cannot smell, taste, touch, see or hear the spiritual so we hesitate to believe it is real.

The Holy Spirit helps us overcome this disunity by promoting the harmony of the physical and the spiritual. At their creation, Adam and Eve's bodies and spirits were in perfect harmony. But at the fall, their bodies took charge and started warring with their spirits. The apostle Paul clearly describes this problem when he claims, "For I do not what I want, but I do the very thing I hate" (Romans 7:15b). Our goal is to become as seamless as possible. As we let the power and life of God flow through us, we become the person he created us to be, and God becomes known to the world through us.

DAY 1

LOVE FOR THE LOST

Scripture of the Day: Luke 15:3-6

Then Jesus told them this parable:

> *"Suppose one of you has a hundred sheep and loses one of them. Doesn't he leave the ninety-nine in the open country and go after the lost sheep until he finds it? And when he finds it, he joyfully puts it on his shoulders and goes home. Then he calls his friends and neighbors together and says, 'Rejoice with me; I have found my lost sheep.'*

Devotional Thought

When my middle daughter was four years old, we took a family trip to Disney. After a fun-filled day, it was time to leave, and she did not understand why. What child ever wants to leave Disney, really? She began to pout and walk slowly as we headed out. I promised her we would come back tomorrow and hugged her as she stood by my leg, but she was not happy.

As we were getting ready to board the tram, I handed my younger son to my oldest daughter. I grabbed the baby bags from the stroller so my husband could fold it, but just as I reached out for my youngest daughter's hand, I realized she was no longer by my side. Fear gripped my heart as I turned toward the park and thought, *how will we ever find her in Disney?*

I screamed as my husband took off running back to the park. It was terrifying as I screamed her name repeatedly. Finally, a woman sitting on the tram said to me, "Is this her?" There she was, sitting on the tram watching the entire family fall apart.

At that moment my heart started to beat again. When Jesus told the parable of the lost sheep, He demonstrated how passionately God feels about those who are lost. Sinners are never forsaken by God. We all sin and go astray just like those sheep. And like a loving mother who thinks she's lost her child in one of the largest amusement parks in the world, God earnestly wants us to be returned to His loving care. Always know your heavenly Father will do all that He can because He wants you to be safe with Him in his loving protection.

Consider this

- How does this apply to my life?

- What I think:

- What I feel:

- What I will do next:

- How can I live a Word-centered life?

DAY 2

GOD CARES FOR YOU

Scripture of the Day: 1 Peter 5:6-7

Humble yourselves, therefore, under God's mighty hand, that he may lift you up in due time. Cast all your anxiety on him because he cares for you.

Devotional Thought

Peter wrote these words likely from Rome during the first century under the reign of Nero. During his lifetime, Peter experienced the fear of political persecution, beatings, jail and threats. Yet, Peter throughout his writings, thanks God for salvation. He shares how he believes one can survive challenging times and bad situations. Peter understood that in order to overcome the challenges of life we need someone greater than us to bear the load of life. Peter offers God as the one we need to cast our cares upon.

Life can leave us filled with anxiety and worry. But in the midst of this we have the promise of God's strength and care. Recently, my email messages would not download. While I am not totally sure what caused the problem, what I do know is that my inbox functioned as if it was on overload and could not download any more emails. When I recognized the issue, it had been five days since I'd received any new messages.

Does life ever feel like that to you? Do feel so overwhelmed by life's challenges that you cannot take another thing? Sometimes it feels easier to shut down. Yet when life puts us on overload and the world's politics, racism, sexism, violence and our own human failures seek to push us to capacity, there is a solution.

First, we must humble ourselves by admitting we can't handle life without God. Next, we must have the correct view of God. He is greater than the weight that often overloads our lives. God can do something about what triggers or tries to defeat us. Finally, we must accept our role in our own relief. We must choose to consistently cast our cares and anxiety on God. Remember, He cares, and He will help us find relief and strength to face our realities with hope and joy. Allow yourself to sit, feel and be affirmed by this unchangeable fact: God cares for you.

Consider this

- How does this apply to my life?

- What I think:

- What I feel:

- What I will do next:

- How can I live a Spirit-empowered life?

DAY 3

ASKING THE RIGHT QUESTIONS

Scripture of the Day: Job 2:9-10

Then his wife said to him, "Do you still hold fast your integrity? Curse God and die!" But he said to her, "You speak as one of the foolish women speaks. Shall we indeed accept good from God and not accept adversity?" In all this Job did not sin with his lips.

Devotional Thought

During times of suffering, we often want to raise a fist at life, at those who caused the suffering and even point a finger at God. We view whatever and whoever may be contributing to the test in our life as an enemy. It is easy to fall into depression, self-pity, and bitterness when we feel as if we are sinking. All of these emotions make it hard to have a new perspective. It is hard to see how the test or suffering is helpful and could make us better. Yet gaining a new perspective or way of seeing life is one of the greatest benefits of tests.

When tests come, they cause us to ask questions of ourselves and others. However, when the *right* question is asked, at the *right* time, with the *right* attitude, it can have a profound impact on our lives. Questions are not accusations, rather they have a way of helping us to see things differently.

Job's wife asked him a question at the onset of his suffering. While his initial response was swift and sharp, it seemed to cause him to think about the test and to consider his wife's question. The next time you are asked a question, before you lash out at the person who asked it, stop, and think. Could God be using that person to help you gain a new perspective? What will your response be?

Consider this

- How does this apply to my life?

- What I think:

- What I feel:

- What I will do next:

- How can I live a Word-centered life?

DAY 4

COMPASSION SOUNDS LIKE THIS

Scripture of the Day: James 3:9-10

> *With the tongue we praise our Lord and Father, and with it we curse human beings, who have been made in God's likeness. Out of the same mouth come praise and cursing. My brothers and sisters, this should not be.*

Devotional Thought

One day in a seminary class, my classmate made a comment that I felt was hurtful. It was the summer of 2020, and the nation was ablaze as a result of the murder of George Floyd in Minneapolis.

Our professor asked us to state the facts that we knew about Mr. Floyd's case. Next, the professor asked us to discuss the ethical challenges surrounding the care of Mr. Floyd and the responsibility of each bystander who witnessed his inhuman and brutal death.

When asked to share the facts we knew and/or understood about the case, one of my classmates began with "I know many of you won't like this" and then stated because we did not know everything about the story there was not a lot, he could say he "knew for sure" about the case.

My stomach sank at hearing his response and my fellow classmates went into an uproar. I think we all trusted the video we saw of the officer's knee on George Floyd's neck for nine minutes. We heard George Floyd stating repeatedly, "I can't breathe" and calling out to his deceased mother. We all trusted that we saw George Floyd's lifeless body on the ground. While we didn't know all the facts, we knew enough facts and so did millions of people around the world who marched, chanted, and prayed for justice.

I was hurt and traumatized. I wanted to lash out but instead, I pursued holiness and measured my response by yielding to the Holy Spirit. This response left my classmate, and more importantly, myself with my dignity intact. The entire class was able to come to order for an insightful, yet passionate discussion.

Is there someone who has hurt or harmed you with their view or perspective? If so, what should your response be? Do you run or engage? How can you engage in a difficult conversation that will show the love of Christ and demonstrate compassion? For 24 hours, tame your tongue. If you must lead with "I know many of you won't like this" it should give you pause. Pray today that you will use your words to heal and not harm others.

Consider this

- How does this apply to my life?

- What I think:

- What I feel:

- How can I live a virtuous and Spirit-empowered life?

DAY 5

SEEING GOD CLEARLY

Scripture of the Day: Isaiah 6:1

In the year of King Uzziah's death I saw the Lord sitting on a throne, lofty and exalted, with the train of His robe filling the temple.

Devotional Thought

Sometimes eyeglasses will have two prescriptions. One to see at a distance and the other to read small print. There is an ideal distance from the glasses and the object in which the focus is perfectly clear. I call this a visual "sweet spot." One day, I held a piece of paper up and much to my frustration I could not focus to read it. I brought the paper in closer, and it became fuzzier. I pulled the paper away and the words still looked fuzzy. It was not until I stopped and focused to ensure that I had the correct distance I needed for my eyes that I was able to see clearly. This can happen in life as well.

Isaiah knew King Uzziah well and in 2 Chronicles 26 we find a full account of Uzziah's life. Some scholars suggest that Isaiah and King Uzziah were related. Certainly, Isaiah had great respect and admiration for King Uzziah. In addition, Isaiah would have been well aware of the accomplishments of King Uzziah's rule. We can learn more from 2 Chronicles 26:1-23 on the life of King Uzziah.

Second Chronicles 26 tells us when Uzziah ruled Judah he experienced great prosperity. Uzziah's fifty-two-year reign was marked by a great and powerful army. Isaiah would have known that Uzziah followed God at a young age and led with His help.

Uzziah acted corruptly, out of pride, one day. He entered the temple of the Lord to burn incense on the altar and was struck with leprosy. However, Isaiah the prophet had great admiration for King Uzziah. For Isaiah to hear of the King's death would have been a sad day. It was a turning point for Isaiah. In the face of his loss, he had a vision and saw the Lord more clearly.

Sometimes, it takes frustration, sadness, or loss to see God more clearly and to gain greater perspective. These types of experiences can be bleak and difficult. However, if we allow ourselves to see through our dilemmas, they can allow us to see God as a reigning Sovereign who is in control of the universe. When your world crumbles, it is good to look at things from heaven's point of view.

Consider this

- How does this apply to my life?

- What I think:

- What I feel:

- What I will do next:

- How can I live the Incarnational life?

DAY 6

SPEAKING ON MY BEHALF

Scripture of the Day: Romans 8:26-27

> *In the same way, the Spirit helps us in our weakness. We do not know what we ought to pray for, but the Spirit himself intercedes for us through wordless groans. And he who searches our hearts knows the mind of the Spirit, because the Spirit intercedes for God's people in accordance with the will of God.*

Devotional Thought

Every week, I moderate a prayer call. My role as the moderator is to welcome everyone to the call and ensure the individuals praying on the call can be heard. I mute callers to ensure it is quiet and that those praying can be heard.

One day, at the end of one of our calls, I unmuted my phone and began to talk. After thanking everyone who joined, I recognized those callers who prayed and the devoted member who organized the call. As I was thanking our guest speaker for offering a timely and compassionate word of encouragement, a voice interrupted me. It was that of our organizer repeating everything I just said.

I was talking but for some reason the callers could not hear me. I was muted. There are times when God speaks and yet we can't hear Him. There are times when we don't have the words to say because our circumstances rob us of words, and we are left with moaning. God is encouraging us to remain saved and keep our faith. Yet when we try to respond to Him, we don't have the words.

Romans 8:26-27 tells us the Holy Spirit translates and intercedes for us so we can talk to God. Had it not been for the call organizer, those callers would have never heard my closing thoughts and blessings. Thank God we have an intercessor, the Holy Spirit, who intercedes for us and offers us an open line of communication to our heavenly Father.

Can you think of a time when you needed the Holy Spirit to intercede for you as you prayed to God? How do you understand the Holy Spirit's work in your life? Today, recognize the Holy Spirit, as He is always interceding for us. The Holy Spirit gives us the words to speak and the faith to rest assured that God speaks to His children.

Consider this

- How does this apply to my life?

- What I think:

- What I feel:

- What I will do next:

- How can I live a Spirit-empowered life?

DAY 7

ALL THINGS ARE WORKING FOR GOOD

Scripture of the Day: Romans 8:28

And we know that in all things God works for the good of those who love him, who have been called according to his purpose.

Devotional Thought

Not too long ago, I celebrated a colleague's birthday on Zoom. I put up a background of a cake with candles and did my best rendition of "Happy Birthday" by Stevie Wonder. My colleague could only see the background that appeared on my screen. In reality, I was sitting in the room with my husband, a cup of coffee in my favorite mug, the ceiling fan was going and so many other things were going on behind the scenes. At first glance, it could appear that I was alone. It wasn't until a few minutes into my greeting with my colleague that my husband joined in and yelled "Happy Birthday." She heard his voice, and it was a welcomed surprise.

Sometimes in life, when we look at what is facing us, it may seem we are alone, even powerless. The book of Romans reminds us that the believer has been freed from sin and has liberty through Christ Jesus. Even when we make mistakes, are filled with guilt, or don't embrace that Christ has set us free from the slavery of sin, we are surrounded by the Lord's loving presence.

In times when we fall, we can restore our relationship with God by confessing and repenting. Even greater, we can rest assured that whatever we face behind the scenes God is working on our behalf and for our good. We only need to invite the Lord into our realities and accept His freedom. We never have to hide who we are from Him. One way we can experience the Lord's reassurance is through prayer. Praying Romans 8:28 is a reminder that God is always working things for the good of His children.

Consider this

- How does this apply to my life?

- What I think:

- What I feel:

- What I will do next:

- How can I live a prayer-filled life?

DAY 8

APPRECIATE THE RAIN

Scripture of the Day: James 1:2

Consider it all joy, my brethren, when you encounter various trials,

Devotional Thought

Recently, a huge storm covered our city with rain, lightning, and wind. I looked down and noticed there was a puddle of water on the floor in my bedroom. Only to look up and see the water slowly dripping from the ceiling. I called a roofer to come out and inspect the roof hoping he'd give us an affordable and fast way to fix it.

When he arrived, he went up on the roof and into the attic to figure out what was going on. Upon the completion of his inspection, he told me what he thought was wrong, but said he wouldn't know for sure and would need to come back on another day. He needed to return because it had stopped raining by the time he arrived.

A few days passed between the time he came back to inspect the roof. He told me he needed to inspect the roof while it was raining because he needed the location of the rain before he could properly identify and solve the problem.

Often, it is in the rainy seasons of life that we identify a problem or a need for a repair. When those days come, it's better to have a God who can help you than to curse the rain. In the rain, we can identify our issues, take them to the Lord in prayer and ask for the help needed.

James was a first century Jewish Christian living in a Gentile community outside of Judea. He wrote to a people who had been scattered throughout the Mediterranean world, endured persecution, trouble, and adversity. The issues for these believers were consistent. Yet James' response was to encourage these Christians to count it all joy. Why? Because when facing trails that tested their faith it highlighted areas for personal discipleship, corporate worship, and growing an immature faith.

Without the trials, these followers of Christ may have been lulled into believing their faith was mature and thriving. Today, I invite you to pray and ask God how your trials can benefit your spiritual growth and lead to deeper faith and joy.

Consider this

- How does this apply to my life?

- What I think:

- What I feel:

- What I will do next:

- How can I live a prayer-filled life?

DAY 9

STAGES OF GRIEF

Scripture of the Day: John 11:17-20

So when Jesus came, He found that he had already been in the tomb four days. Now Bethany was near Jerusalem, about two miles off; and many of the Jews had come to Martha and Mary, to console them concerning their brother. Martha therefore, when she heard that Jesus was coming, went to meet Him, but Mary stayed at the house.

Devotional Thought

During the 2020 COVID-19 pandemic, the nation watched in horror as human beings around the world lost family, friends and associates. Children were left orphaned; young newlyweds were left widowed; and best friends separated far too soon. Even more tragic was the inability to funeralize family and bring closure in familiar ways.

Many people still grieve today and will for a very long time. Among these losses were also jobs, businesses, homes, and plans for the future.

According to Elisabeth Kubler-Ross, there are five stages of grief She describes them as **Denial** (this can't be happening), **Anger** (why did this happen and who is to blame?), **Bargaining** (make this not happen and I

will do whatever to make it go away), **Depression** (I can't bear this; I'm too sad to do anything), and **Acceptance** (I acknowledge that this has happened, and I cannot change it.)

These stages do not occur in a linearly and some stages may never occur or will occur for only a short time. Whatever you are grieving today, allow yourself the time to grieve. This includes creating safe places in your life to grieve, spending time in prayer, and reading the Scripture such as Psalm 18:32-36. Seek the support you need to grieve.

In John 11:17-20, Lazarus' sisters decide how they want to grieve his death. Mary rose and quickly engaged Jesus while Martha remained in the house. In whatever way you grieve, please give yourself the gift of grieving. Jesus will meet every one of your needs as you do.

Consider this

- How does this apply to my life?

- What I think:

- What I feel:

- What I will do next:

- How can I live a prayer-filled life?

DAY 10

GOOD TROUBLE

Scripture of the Day: John 18:19-24

The high priest then questioned Jesus about His disciples, and about His teaching. Jesus answered him, "I have spoken openly to the world; I always taught in synagogues and in the temple, where all the Jews come together; and I spoke nothing in secret. "Why do you question Me? Question those who have heard what I spoke to them; they know what I said." When He had said this, one of the officers standing nearby struck Jesus, saying, "Is that the way You answer the high priest?" Jesus answered him, "If I have spoken wrongly, testify of the wrong; but if rightly, why do you strike Me?" So Annas sent Him bound to Caiaphas the high priest.

Devotional Thought

John Lewis said, "Do not get lost in a sea of despair. Be hopeful, be optimistic. Our struggle is not the struggle of a day, a week, a month, or a year, it is the struggle of a lifetime. Never, ever be afraid to make some noise and get in good trouble, necessary trouble."

John Lewis challenged generations with these words. As a young man, he fought tirelessly for civil rights. Along with being unjustly beaten, he

was jailed often. As a young boy, his parents told him not to get into trouble. But as he grew into a civil rights leader, he realized there are some types of trouble we should get into.

In this passage in John 18, Jesus demonstrated a model of getting into good trouble. Speaking truth to power, dedicating one's life to justice, and drawing others to wholeness in God through a personal relationship is how Jesus described His actions. Jesus did not use force in His rebuttals or in life; He used truth.

Do you have an opportunity to change the lives of others? Will you accept this opportunity and use truth as your means to do so?

Consider this

- How does this apply to my life?

- What I think:

- What I feel:

- What I will do next:

- How can I live a compassionate life?

DAY 11

GOD IS PRESENT

Scripture of the Day: Psalm 46:1

God is our refuge and strength, A very present help in trouble.

Devotional Thought

Psalm 46:1 was written as a hymn of triumph and celebration to God for being a present help, a deliverer, and protector. It is said that the descendants of Korah who were temple musicians wrote this Psalm. Other scholars write that the occasion that caused the writing of this Psalm was the deliverance of Jerusalem from Moab and Ammon during the reign of Jehoshaphat. Another thought is that this Psalm was connected to Sennacherib's abandonment of the siege of Jerusalem in the time of Hezekiah's reign (2 Kings 18:13-19:37). Whatever the occasion, one theme is clear: God is always there.

One day, I had to take my car to the dealership, and they gave me a loaner car. The loaner was a hybrid and one of its features is that the car would go into a "green" state whenever the car sat idle. This meant the engine would not emit harmful fumes. While I appreciate the technology, when the car powered down it would be so quiet, I thought it had cut off. However, every time I hit the gas it would power up and move.

Have you ever felt like God was not working in your life; almost as if He is so quiet and powered down that you were not sure if He would be able to carry you into your next season? Well, the Scripture is clear. Even when it seems God is not working, He is. He doesn't take naps. He won't break down on you and He always has the power to get you to where you need to be.

Consider this

- How does this apply to my life?

- What I think:

- What I feel:

- What I will do next:

- How can I live a prayer-filled life?

DAY 12

AN UNCONVENTIONAL FAITH

Scripture of the Day: Mark 5:25-29

> And a woman was there who had been subject to bleeding for twelve years. She had suffered a great deal under the care of many doctors and had spent all she had, yet instead of getting better she grew worse. When she heard about Jesus, she came up behind him in the crowd and touched his cloak, because she thought, "If I just touch his clothes, I will be healed." Immediately her bleeding stopped and she felt in her body that she was freed from her suffering.

Devotional Thought

Howie Kendrick, a first base player for the Washington Nationals is a 2019 World Series champion. He once said, "there is no success without effort or error."

One of the scariest things to face in life is a problem with no solution. These types of situations often require unconventional action. We often exhaust ourselves by doing the same things and getting the same results instead of going to Jesus.

In the story of the woman who struggled with the issue of blood, she did just that, and the results were miraculous. Considered ceremonially unclean as described in Leviticus 15:25, this woman should not have been in public, let alone putting forth the effort to touch Jesus. Jesus was moved by unconventional acts of faith, and he responded positively. This unconventional act of faith is a reminder that it is safe to trust the Lord over human effort and understanding.

We often push away feelings of desperation and fear. However, these are the very feelings we should explore because they push us closer to Jesus. Is there something you need but you've tried everything on your own to meet that need? If you were not afraid, what would you do? Ask the Lord to guide your steps. God has never given us fear but rather power, love, and a sound mind. It may be time for an unconventional act of faith.

Consider this

- How does this apply to my life?

- What I think:

- What I feel:

- What I will do next:

- How can I live a Spirit-empowered life?

DAY 13

I KNOW WHO I AM

Scripture of the Day: 1 John 3:1-3

See what love the Father has given us, that we should be called children of God; and that is what we are. The reason the world does not know us is that it did not know him. Beloved, we are God's children now; what we will be has not yet been revealed. What we do know is this: when he is revealed, we will be like him, for we will see him as he is. And all who have this hope in him purify themselves, just as he is pure.

Devotional Thought

The apostle John writes these words to encourage several Gentile congregations between AD 85-90. Written prior to being banished to the island of Patmos, this eyewitness account of the ministry of Christ wrote extensively about love and God's family. He often stressed that we become God's children by believing in Jesus Christ. Further still, this belief allows us to love other believers and live as loving family members.

As a result of God's love, we have the unimaginable capacity to demonstrate this love to others, even when we have traveled different paths in life. Our ethnicity, race, gender or sexual orientation do not exclude us from embracing our identity as a child of God and loving one another and Jesus Christ. We can hold onto our belief in Christ and God's love as these offers present-day hope and a bright future. God will transform us to become reflections of His love day by day. And one great day we will see Jesus Christ face to face and any struggles we have had with loving others or understanding who we are will be gone. We will stand in the pure light and love of Christ.

Consider this

- How does this apply to my life?

- What I think:

- What I feel:

- What I will do next:

- How can I live a compassionate life?

DAY 14

THE POWER OF CONTENTMENT

Scripture of the Day: Philippians 4:12-13

I can do all things through Him who strengthens me.

Devotional Thought

One of the biggest dangers to believers is entitlement. This entitlement feeds the idea of prosperity which teaches us that we must be rich, healthy, and have the newest car, house, and clothing. It also tells us when we don't have these things or a desired status that something is wrong with us or even worse, that something is wrong with God. As a result, we lack contentment.

When I was a child I would tell my mom on Christmas Eve, "I can't wait until tomorrow!" She would reply, "I bet you can." As an excited child, I hated this response. However, she was right. There is no way I could speed up time. I had to learn to be content with Christmas Eve while waiting for Christmas Day.

Paul knew what it was like to be locked into a present situation that was anything but ideal. He understood what it meant to look forward to a new and brighter day. Yet as Paul sat in a Roman prison, he wrote to the church in Philippi to share his gratitude and joy. He had started the church on his second missionary journey (Acts 16:11-40). Paul had lived a life of great wealth and great poverty. However, he always remained content wherever he found himself after his conversion. So, it is no surprise that Paul could say these words because his contentment and joy sprang from a life dedicated to serving God and others.

Material things, money nor status can give us lasting joy. Only a relationship with God through Jesus Christ and a life of service to others can do this. The next time you find yourself feeling unsatisfied, envious of others, or anxious about your next success, ask God to help you focus on the eternal. Ask God to help you understand what you are called to do and find contentment in that. It takes courage to accept God's priorities for your life above what you think you should own or be. He can transform our hearts when we decide to seek and practice contentment.

Consider this

- How does this apply to my life?

- What I think:

- What I feel:

- What I will do next:

- How can I live a prayer-filled life?

DAY 15

FAITH TO GO FORWARD

Scripture of the Day: Ruth 1:16-18

> *But Ruth replied, "Don't urge me to leave you or to turn back from you. Where you go I will go, and where you stay I will stay. Your people will be my people and your God my God. Where you die I will die, and there I will be buried. May the LORD deal with me, be it ever so severely, if even death separates you and me." When Naomi realized that Ruth was determined to go with her, she stopped urging her.*

Devotional Thought

When I drive from Virginia to the Dover Airforce base in Delaware, I have to drive across the long and massive Chesapeake Bay Bridge. Imagine being surrounded by steel, water and clouds for miles and miles. As I drive toward the Chesapeake Bay Bridge, I get anxious just knowing what awaits. I am not alone in my fears. People park at the foot of the bridge, and for a sizable fee, will offer to drive cars over for those who cannot stand the sight of the bridge and drive across it themselves. I would imagine the fear of the known, but accept if I didn't drive forward, I would never reach my goal.

The decision to move forward is exemplified in the life of Ruth. Widows in ancient Israelite culture were vulnerable in a male-dominated society. Not only was Ruth a widow and childless, but she would now be a foreigner as she declared allegiance to her mother-in-law and followed her from Judah to Bethlehem.

Ruth's story unfolds as she marries Boaz, a respected man who lived in Bethlehem. Ruth's willingness to move forward would one day result in her becoming the great-grandmother of King David. Through loyalty to Naomi, faith and hope in God and her cleverness and ingenuity Ruth's once dark and scary life produced beautiful outcomes. Ruth made it to the other side of her crisis, and you can too. What situation are you facing that seems scary and insurmountable? How can your faith help you to move forward?

Consider this

- How does this apply to my life?

- What I think:

- What I feel:

- What I will do next:

- How can I live a prayer filled and virtuous life?

DAY 16

BECAUSE I'M HAPPY!

Scripture of the Day: Acts 26:26

For the king knows about these things, and to him I speak boldly. For I am persuaded that none of these things has escaped his notice, for this has not been done in a corner.

Devotional Thought

At the end of one of the many virtual school days, I asked my children, "How was your day?" This was day three of virtual school due to the COVID-19 pandemic. They answered, "Boring." They exclaimed how they don't get to talk to anyone and can only listen to the teacher. It was obvious this temporary way of learning lost its excitement for my children fast.

But this was never the case for Paul and his conversion. In Acts 26, we meet the apostle Paul who is standing before King Agrippa. He is defending his devotion to Judaism, and how passionate he was after his conversion, preaching the gospel and living a life of obedience and sacrifice to ministry. Paul had been accused of wrongdoing but declares his innocence.

King Agrippa agrees that he could not support any charges. The beauty however is that in the face of false and unsubstantiated charges, Paul delights in telling his salvation story. Paul's conversion never grew old. He was always excited to share the gospel and his story of conversion to Jesus Christ with others.

Consider this

- How does this apply to my life?

- What I think:

- What I feel:

- What I will do next:

- How can I live a Word-centered life?

DAY 17

MY LIVING IS NOT VAIN

Scripture of the Day: Nehemiah 6:3

And I sent messengers to them, saying, "I am doing a great work and I cannot come down. Why should the work stop while I leave it and come down to you?"

Devotional Thought

"If I Can Help Somebody" was sung by the great Mahalia Jackson who was an American gospel singer. She was referred to as "the Queen of Gospel" and became one of the most influential gospel singers in the world. Most notably, she was recognized internationally as a singer and civil rights activist. The lyrics capture the thought of one who recognizes that serving and fulfilling the work God created them to do is a great value and should continue.

In this scripture, Nehemiah recognized that he was being tempted by Sanballat to stop the work and progress he was making to rebuild the wall. Nehemiah demonstrates to us that whatever God has called us to do is important, and has value to God and we should value it as well. Even when days are long and challenges arise, remember to always view your work as meaningful and don't let distractors devalue what you're doing.

In the words of Mahalia Jackson, your living will not be in vain.

If I can help somebody, as I travel along
If I can help somebody, with a word or song
If I can help somebody, from doing wrong
No, my living shall not be in vain.

No, my living shall not be in vain
No, my living shall not be in vain
If I can help somebody, as I'm singing the song
You know, my living shall not be in vain.

Consider this

- How does this apply to my life?

- What I think:

- What I feel:

- What I will do next:

- How can I live a compassionate and prayer-filled life?

DAY 18

MANAGING STRESS

Scripture of the Day: Psalm 90:1-2

> *Lord, you have been our dwelling place throughout all generations. Before the mountains were born or you brought forth the whole world, from everlasting to everlasting you are God.*

Devotional Thought

In his book, *Why Zebras Don't Get Ulcers*, Robert M. Sapolsky examines the topic of stress and what we can learn from zebras. Zebras live in the wild and are often exposed to danger as they are hunted by other animals and often have to endure living in harsh elements. However, zebras seem to demonstrate an ability to manage stress and bounce back given their environment.

By studying zebras and other mammals, Sapolsky has drawn some conclusions about human beings. He suggests two of the reasons we often experience stress is because of a lack of predictability and a lack of control in life. Life is filled with sharp turns and deep shifts from day to day. Predictability makes stressors less stressful. When we can predict what is coming and believe we have some control over our response, the stress decreases. But how can we do this?

Moses wrote a thought in Psalm 90 that offers us both predictability and control. In Psalm 90 we are reminded that we serve an eternal God who created and is in control of the world and all living in it. Greater still is the fact that as a child of God, we can live and find safety in Him. What are you facing that you did not expect to happen? What part of your life feels beyond your control? Take it to God and allow Him to replace the stress with peace.

Consider this

- How does this apply to my life?

- What I think:

- What I feel:

- What I will do next:

- How can I live a prayer-filled and Spirit-empowered life?

DAY 19

A GOOD WORK IN YOU

Scripture of the Day: Philippians 1:6-7

For I am confident of this very thing, that He who began a good work in you will perfect it until the day of Christ Jesus. For it is only right for me to feel this way about you all, because I have you in my heart, since both in my imprisonment and in the defense and confirmation of the gospel, you all are partakers of grace with me.

Devotional Thought

The apostle Paul wrote the book of Philippians from a prison in Rome. Despite Paul's trials and troubles, one of the major themes in the book of Philippians is joy and his love for the Christian community at Philippi. It was the Philippians who gave Paul financial help and support when he was in Philippi and in prison. Because of this Paul understood the truth that God's work in our individual lives and the lives we live together is how we are transformed to be more like Christ each day.

When we partner with others and help others through prayer, financial gifts, kindness, and hospitality we are being transformed by God. Your spiritual growth is not achieved by being alone and isolated. Growth and discipleship are achieved by living among others and allowing God to

mature and complete you. God will never stop working to help you become more like Christ.

God's love is always extended to His children even in light of our shortcomings, failures, and feelings of insignificance. Feeling as if you don't measure up? Rest assured that if you turn to God, He will transform your heart to become more like Him each day.

Consider this

- How does this apply to my life?

- What I think:

- What I feel:

- What I will do next:

- How can I live a Spirit-empowered and virtuous life?

DAY 20

PRAYING IN DISCOURAGING TIMES

Scripture of the Day: 1 Samuel 1:15-16

"Not so, my lord," Hannah replied, "I am a woman who is deeply troubled. I have not been drinking wine or beer; I was pouring out my soul to the LORD. Do not take your servant for a wicked woman; I have been praying here out of my great anguish and grief."

Devotional Thought

Hannah, whose name means *favor*, was a woman deep in sorrow. She lived during a time when becoming a mother and wife meant having personal value and status in society. It was also thought to be a sign that God especially favored the women who birthed a son.

Hannah was barren and while she was the favored wife, her husband had another wife, Peninnah, who bore him sons. But she was not a kind person, she taunted and tormented Hannah about her barrenness. Crushed by her realities, Hannah cried out to God in prayer. She allowed her disappointment and raw emotions to lead her to prayer.

Hannah was transformed through prayer in four essential ways. First, she remained aware of her struggles but never sought revenge toward

Peninnah or God. Second, she was present in her struggle. She understood the full weight of the implications, but she had hope and continued to pray.

Third, Hannah did not isolate herself and was able to hear words of comfort and encouragement. While praying in the temple, she had a conversation with Eli, the priest, and his word helped to heal her broken heart. Finally, after praying for some time, she found joy. Life comes in season. Hannah accepted that the time of mourning was finished. It was time for her to eat and trust God by moving forward. Hannah allowed herself to experience God's provision for her immediate physical need and her future heart's desire (a child). Don't ever stop praying especially in hard times.

Consider this

- How does this apply to my life?

- What I think:

- What I feel:

- What I will do next:

- How can I practice the contemplative life?

DAY 21

A GOOD RESPONSE

Scripture of the Day: Job 2:9-10

Then his wife said to him, "Do you still hold fast your integrity? Curse God and die!" But he said to her, "You speak as one of the foolish women speaks. Shall we indeed accept good from God and not accept adversity?" In all this Job did not sin with his lips.

Devotional Thought

In the story of Job, the first few chapters reveal that he is met with one calamity after another. He lost his children, his property, his health, and his status in a short space of time. When we are introduced to Job, we find a man who is described as blameless, upright, and someone who feared God.

Job would get up early in the morning to offer burnt offerings to the Lord for his children. He loved his sons and daughters dearly. The Bible describes that when Job had feasts at his home, his sons and daughters had their places at the table. Job was very concerned with the condition of the heart and demonstrates to the believer that health and wealth are not evidence of obedience or signs of God's blessings.

Job's life also shows us that suffering and hard times are not a sign of moral failure. Both the saint and the sinner will experience both. However, in suffering, the believer can expect to experience God's grace, love, attention, restoration, compassion, and healing.

In chapter 2 of the book of Job, Job's wife asked him a hard question. She begins to stir up a tension in Job that makes him uncomfortable, even irritated with her. This hard question causes Job to become in tune with the magnitude of his loss and to refocus his attention on what God could be doing in his life. This pushes Job to begin a journey that ultimately proves his faith in God because he knows God is faithful.

Has God used someone to ask you a hard question? If so, before you respond in anger or feel betrayed, pause a moment and consider if what is in your heart matches what you say from your mouth. Your answer may be the springboard for a season of growth.

Consider this

- How does this apply to my life?

- What I think:

- What I feel:

- What I will do next:

- How can I practice living a more Spirit-empowered life?

DAY 22

POWER OF TEARS

Scripture of the Day: John 11:32-35

Now when Mary came to where Jesus was and saw him, she fell at his feet, saying to him, "Lord, if you had been here, my brother would not have died." When Jesus saw her weeping, and the Jews who had come with her also weeping, he was deeply moved in his spirit and greatly troubled. And he said, "Where have you laid him?" They said to him, "Lord, come and see." Jesus wept.

Devotional Thought

H. Norman Wright says this about tears, "when words fail, tears are the messenger." Tears are God's gift to all of us to release our feelings. During moments of loss and grief, I have often held onto the fact that Christ is tender, sympathetic toward me, and understands my tears. Each tear you cry for the death of a loved one, the loss of a job, or a disappointment in life matters to God. He is never overwhelmed by our tears or the situations that cause us to cry.

When Jesus arrived after Lazarus' death, Mary, his sister, met Him and wept. Not only Mary, but the Jews who had gathered to comfort her wept with her. When Jesus arrived at the tomb where Lazarus was buried, He also wept. Even though Jesus knew Lazarus would be raised from the dead, His power did not overshadow His compassion or love for those impacted by grief.

We live in a society where we have become so divided. We barely notice or have allowed our hearts to become hardened and don't care about the sorrows of others. Let this beautiful act of Jesus' compassion remind you that He cares for you deeply. As a result, we should also care for others just as deeply.

Consider this

- How does this apply to my life?

- What I think:

- What I feel:

- What I will do next:

- How can I practice having a more Word-centered life?

DAY 23

IN THE RIGHT PLACE

Scripture of the Day: Colossians 3:1-2

> *Since, then, you have been raised with Christ, set your hearts on things above, where Christ is, seated at the right hand of God. Set your minds on things above, not on earthly things.*

Devotional Thought

As Christians, we sometimes tend to rank sin. We think in terms of little sins versus big sins. We find ourselves hyper-focused on sins committed in the body while we ignore sins of the heart and mind. We often miss or ignore sins that grieve the Holy Spirit. Sexual sins such as adultery are just as destructive as structural evils such as injustice and social sins such as bigotry and psychological manipulation. So, it is no surprise that Paul instructs the believers in Colossae to set their hearts and minds above with Jesus Christ as he stands above all as the life-giving source of the Church.

Paul wanted the Church to understand that newness of life requires us to live in right relationship with Christ and with one another. To Paul, there was no time to rank, only time to rid ourselves of sin that cause us to miss the exalted position of Christ. Because of Christ, our life in Him as believers should cause us to be better and live at a higher standard in word and action. This passage of Scripture lists sinful and negative behaviors that are the result of a heart and mind that is not raised above earthly influences. Each day, we are called to see that Jesus Christ stands over and above our earthly nature and real or perceived power.

Where do your heart and mind need to be raised? Ask Christ to help you to set your heart and mind above things today.

Consider this

- How does this apply to my life?

- What I think:

- What I feel:

- What I will do next:

- How can I practice a virtuous life?

DAY 24

GOD IS "THERE" WITH YOU

Scripture of the Day: Genesis 16:7-11

The angel of the Lord found Hagar near a spring in the desert; it was the spring that is beside the road to Shur. And he said, "Hagar, slave of Sarai, where have you come from, and where are you going?" "I'm running away from my mistress Sarai," she answered. Then the angel of the Lord told her, "Go back to your mistress and submit to her." The angel added, "I will increase your descendants so much that they will be too numerous to count." The angel of the Lord also said to her: "You are now pregnant, and you will give birth to a son. You shall name him Ishmael, for the Lord has heard of your misery.

Devotional Thought

The Danish theologian, Søren Kierkegaard said, "Life can only be understood backwards; but it must be lived forward." Kierkegaard reminds us that as we are living, we are becoming and learning more about who we are and who God is. If we are going to fully engage in becoming and making choices that reflect our desire to understand God and His work in our lives, we will need to develop a deep and abiding faith in Him, especially given the messiness of life and ministry.

Hagar can attest to the messiness of one's life journey. Hagar, an Egyptian slave girl, found herself living in a time and culture in the Near East where it was not uncommon for a married infertile woman to offer her female servant to her husband to produce offspring. While 21st-century medical technology would cause us to cringe at this type of arrangement, this was a common practice.

So, as Hagar carried the child Sarai longed to carry, something in the way Sarai experienced her bareness and something in the way Hagar claimed equality with Sarai as she carried her baby led to these words being recorded to describe the tension that existed between the two women. "She (Hagar) began to despise her mistress." As a result, Sarai's mistreatment of Hagar and the desired but absent intervention from Abram, led her to risk death by running away into the desert, alone, unprotected, and unprepared. She runs away to escape the wrath of Sarai.

Life can hit like a tsunami. It is hard to make sense of God's timing, to experience His love, to see Him as generous, just, powerful, or trustworthy. We all have had days when we wanted to be anywhere else but where we were. Seeing young children die due to gun violence, learning that young people filled with promise die by suicide, all while living in the context of a pandemic can feel like life is crumbling beneath us.

Yet, this Egyptian slave woman teaches us that the child of God does not have to run from life's realities, nor its triumphs (Hagar is pregnant) and its tragedies (harsh treatment from someone who is in a position to bless you) to seek relief. Hagar teaches us that if you do "run," God will meet you "there," wherever you stop running because He is present in our crises. God gives us the strength to face our realities and the humility to return to some situations and see His power and ability to provide. Allow God to lovingly set you on a new course. It begins with meeting Him in prayer.

Consider this

- How does this apply to my life?

- What I think:

- What I feel:

- What I will do next:

- How can I practice the contemplative life?

DAY 25

SURVIVING THE STORM

Scripture of the Day: Matthew 8:23-27

When He got into the boat, His disciples followed Him. And behold, there arose a great storm on the sea, so that the boat was being covered with the waves; but Jesus Himself was asleep. And they came to Him and woke Him, saying, "Save us, Lord; we are perishing!" He *said to them, "Why are you afraid, you men of little faith?" Then He got up and rebuked the winds and the sea, and it became perfectly calm. The men were amazed, and said, "What kind of a man is this, that even the winds and the sea obey Him?"

Devotional Thought

The start of this decade has been unbelievable. While many have been blessed to get married and have babies, others have experienced significant loss and trauma. From a pandemic to record-breaking unemployment and civil unrest to an extremely negative election season, many people have had to weather the storms of life head-on.

In life, we will find ourselves in the middle of storms. The waves of life crash into us and we find ourselves unprepared and overwhelmed.

However, we can cry out, "Save us, Lord," just like the disciples who traveled with Jesus on that day when the storm occurred.

Recently, a hurricane was headed toward my city. In the days leading up to the arrival of the storm I bought water, watched the weather reports, and even packed my emergency bag. However, I never moved the patio furniture into the garage. It was not until I heard the rain, wind, and noise of flapping umbrellas and sliding patio furniture, did I realize my patio furniture might be blown away.

At that moment, I thought WHY. In all of my planning, I still found myself confronted with the unexpected. Only fast action, some help from my son, my trusty rain boots and jacket, and a quick prayer could save me now. In that moment, I was reminded the storms of life arise and while we should expect some of them, we are never fully prepared for many of them. In those moments, cry out to the Lord. Whether your cry is fueled by fear or faith, use the storms of life to experience the Lord's miracle working power.

In the end, you will find that Jesus can calm what rages in your life and anything that would attempt to toss you around has to obey His commands. Have you experienced unexpected trials or challenges recently? How is the Lord calming the storms in your life?

Consider this

- How does this apply to my life?

- What I think:

- What I feel:

- What I will do next:

- How can I practice a prayer-filled life?

DAY 26

NATURE'S REMINDER

Scripture of the Day: Psalm 23:1-3

> *The LORD is my shepherd; I shall not want. He maketh me to lie down in green pastures: he leadeth me beside the still waters. He restoreth my soul: he leadeth me in the paths of righteousness for his name's sake.*

Devotional Thought

One of the many things we can appreciate about David is his connection with nature. He was a phenomenal leader, military strategist, shepherd, musician and poet but he also had many challenges in life.

David dealt with Saul who was jealous of him and attempted to have him killed more than once. Absalom, his son, turned against his father and sought to take over his throne. David also had moral failures in his personal life that included adultery and the murder of an innocent man. Yet, in all of this, David demonstrated gratitude and was always open with God about what was going on in his life.

One of the many ways David stayed anchored and maintained a healthy mind, spirit, and connection to God was through nature. Those years as a shepherd tending sheep by streams of water allowed David to quiet his soul and tune into God. In Psalm 29, in the middle of a storm, David heard the voice of the Lord through the storm. When life hurries us and causes us to feel frantic, one of the best things we can do is step outside and experience nature. When is the last time you took a walk, sat on your porch or stood on your balcony and felt the sun, listened to the birds, or watched the breeze move the leaves on a tree? Experiencing God through nature can be a wonderful way to care for your soul and connect with God.

Consider this

- How does this apply to my life?

- What I think:

- What I feel:

- What I will do next:

- How can I practice the incarnational life.

DAY 27

BECOMING MORE MERCIFUL

Scripture for the Day: Ephesians 4:32

Be kind and compassionate to one another, forgiving each other, just as in Christ God forgave you.

Devotional Thought

In the book of Ephesians, Paul challenges his reader to apply their faith in a very practical way. He encouraged the early church believers to walk in unity, humility, and gentleness as a lifestyle. It seems as if whenever there was a lack of harmony in relationships, pride, unkindness, and a lack of respect existed.

Paul affirms that in life we will experience the negativity of others. For whatever reason, there will be days when we are on the receiving end of someone's disappointment, anger, and frustration. Instead of finding ways to regulate these emotions, some individuals choose to lash out. That is where we will need to make a conscious decision on what response will be used to address others.

Ephesians 4:32 teaches us how to respond. We should expect to experience bullies, insensitive comments, or rudeness. What will give life and longevity to these behaviors is how we decide to respond. The greatest gift we can give ourselves and others are to be kind, compassionate and forgiving. What can motivate us to extend ourselves in this way is a short recall and a long memory. Easily forgetting the offenses and never forgetting God's forgiveness was extended to us and must be offered to others.

Consider this

- How does this apply to my life?

- What I think:

- What I feel:

- What I will do next:

- How can I practice the incarnational life?

DAY 28

LITTLE GRACES ALL AROUND

Scripture for the Day: Philippians 4:8

Finally, brethren, whatever is true, whatever is honorable, whatever is right, whatever is pure, whatever is lovely, whatever is of good repute, if there is any excellence and if anything worthy of praise, dwell on these things.

Devotional Thought

In a meditation by theologian Howard Thurman, he wrote, "It is just as important as ever to attend to the little graces by which the dignity of our lives is maintained and sustained. Birds still sing; the stars continue to cast their gentle gleam over the desolation of the battlefields, and the heart is still inspired by the kind word and the gracious deed. In the era when our eyes have collectively witnessed the killing of Sandra Bland, George Floyd and all types of violence, we may feel overwhelmed by grief and fear. It is the little graces that remind us that while our world disintegrates externally, we don't have to internally."

The holiness tradition reminds us that we can have pure thoughts, words, and actions and overcome temptation. We can think of those thoughts which are pure and good instead of falling victim to suspicion, doubt, and cynicism. Before we give up, throw our hands in the air and scream "Things will never change," we should turn to God's word for comfort and direction. Looking up to accuse God should slip away to gratitude and hope. When we think of holiness we must include our thoughts, attitudes, and outlook. Paul encourages us to "think on these things." Our thinking is right, our vision can be clear, and we can maintain energy, power and patience we need to serve God and others even in the face of challenges.

Consider this

- How does this apply to my life?

- What I think:

- What I feel:

- What I will do next:

- How can I practice the virtuous life?

DAY 29

USING YOUR GIFTS FOR OTHERS

Scripture for the Day: Romans 12:4-11

> Scripture for the Day: Romans 12:4-11 *For just as we have many parts in one body and all the body's parts do not have the same function, so we, who are many, are one body in Christ, and individually parts of one another. However, since we have gifts that differ according to the grace given to us, each of us is to use them properly: if prophecy, in proportion to one's faith; if service, in the act of serving; or the one who teaches, in the act of teaching; or the one who exhorts, in the work of exhortation; the one who gives, with generosity; the one who is in leadership, with diligence; the one who shows mercy, with cheerfulness. Love must be free of hypocrisy. Detest what is evil; cling to what is good. Be devoted to one another in brotherly love; give preference to one another in honor, not lagging behind in diligence, fervent in spirit, serving the Lord;*

Devotional Thought

God has given each of us at least one gift. No one has all the gifts. Yet, we find ourselves frustrated when we are confronted with a limitation or weakness. The Holy Spirit has given us exactly the gift or mix of gifts we should have to walk in our God-given purpose and calling.

When we are envious of the gifts others have and doubt our dreams or callings will ever come to pass, we really are doubting the sovereignty of God. These gifts are to be used to bring harmony between our daily lives and our faith. Look at the life of Christ. We are called to connect with people. Our family, friends, and neighbors are often the people we start connecting with first. However, through work, play, volunteering, and service we can connect with others and use our gifts to serve them.

Consider this

- How does this apply to my life?

- What I think:

- What I feel:

- What I will do next:

- How can I practice the Spirit-empowered and incarnational life?

DAY 30

GOD'S WAY TO GET YOU TO MOVE

Scripture for the Day: Joshua 1:1-3

Now it came about after the death of Moses the servant of the LORD, that the LORD spoke to Joshua the son of Nun, Moses' servant, saying, "Moses My servant is dead; now therefore arise, cross this Jordan, you and all this people, to the land which I am giving to them, to the sons of Israel. "Every place on which the sole of your foot treads, I have given it to you, just as I spoke to Moses.

Devotional Thought

Stop by any playground and you will see children with their mothers or father helping them to negotiate playground politics. The child is taken to the edge of the playground, and never having played here before, they must figure out how to pierce what seems to be an invisible wall.

Peering over the mulch and standing close to their parent or older sibling, the child watches the other children play, swing, and chase each other. Then without a thought, they feel a gentle nudge and a voice that says, "Go ahead, it will be all right."

That scene continues to be played out in the life of every adult who has faith in God. Those "gentle nudges" often come just in time. Just as we are about to quit and charge God foolishly for bringing something into our lives that is too hard. The gentle nudge is often a nagging dream, an interpersonal conflict that challenges our assumptions. In the moment, the gentle nudge can feel like a hard push that takes our breath and lifts our feet off the ground because we are angry, frustrated, and caught unaware. However, we must not focus all of our energy on how God gets us to move. Rather the focus should be on God's loving involvement in our lives and His desire for our transformation into His image.

When Moses died, it was time for Joshua to arise and lead. God spoke to Joshua and told him to "cross this Jordan." Joshua may have been looking at the Jordan as God was speaking or likely was already familiar with the Jordan. However, as lovingly as a parent gently nudges a child and assures them that they will be right there with them, God demonstrates His power and love. God assures Joshua that the command to cross the Jordan in spite of what he faces is right. Why? Because God will give him the land and all he needs to possess it, just like He promised Moses. God gave Joshua the gift of leadership and he was called to use it in this grand moment.

Consider this

- How does this apply to my life?

- What I think:

- What I feel:

- What I will do next:

- How can I practice the Spirit-filled life?

DAY 31

LIVING A WHOLE LIFE

Scripture for the Day: Luke 9:12-17

Now the day was ending, and the twelve came and said to Him, "Send the crowd away, that they may go into the surrounding villages and countryside and find lodging and get something to eat; for here we are in a desolate place." But He said to them, "You give them something to eat!" And they said, "We have no more than five loaves and two fish, unless perhaps we go and buy food for all these people." (For there were about five thousand men.) And He said to His disciples, "Have them sit down to eat in groups of about fifty each." They did so, and had them all sit down. Then He took the five loaves and the two fish, and looking up to heaven, He blessed them, and broke them, and kept giving them to the disciples to set before the people. And they all ate and were satisfied; and the broken pieces which they had left over were picked up, twelve baskets full.

Devotional Thought

The life of Jesus offers a well-balanced example of how God wants to move in the life of His children. Compassion toward all people, devotion to God, preaching the Good News, being empowered by the Spirit, harmony between faith, work, and service, and virtuous living are evident in the life of Jesus and should be evident in our lives as well.

Think about these areas and assess how fully you are living. The goal is not perfection, but rather balance. If there is an area that is flat refer to the chart, meditate on those Scriptures, and ask God to help you become more robust in that area of life.

Consider this

🍃 How does this apply to my life?

🍃 What I think:

🍃 What I feel:

🍃 What I will do next:

🍃 How can I live a virtuous life?

BIBLIOGRAPHY

Brauch, Manfred T., Abusing Scripture: The Consequences of Misreading the Bible. Downers Grove: IVP Academic, 2009

Foster, Richard J., Streams of Living Water: Celebrate the Great Traditions of Christian Faith. San Francisco: Harper Collins, 1998

Kubler-Ross, Elizabeth. On Death and Dying: What the Dying Have to Teach Doctors, Nurses, Clergy and Their Own Families. New York: Scribner, 1969

Smith, James B., A Spiritual Formation Workbook - Small Group Resources for Nurturing Christian Growth, A Revised edition. New York: Harper Collins, 1999

Sapolsky, Robert M., Why Zebras Don't Get Ulcers: The Acclaimed Guide to Stress, Stress Related Diseases and Coping, Third Edition. New York: St. Martin's Griffin, 2004

Thurman, Howard., Meditations of the Heart. New York: Harper & Row, 1953

Wright, H. Norman., Recovering from Losses in Life. Grand Rapids: Revell, 2006

Unless otherwise indicated, all Scriptures come from the New International Version 2011; New American Standard Bible 1995, the King James Version 2015, English Standard Version, 2001 or the New Revised Standard Version 1989

www.ingramcontent.com/pod-product-compliance
Lightning Source LLC
Chambersburg PA
CBHW030154100526
44592CB00009B/266